Cool Crafts with
Cloth

Jane Yates

WINDMILL BOOKS

Published in 2018 by **Windmill Books**,
an Imprint of Rosen Publishing
29 East 21st Street, New York, NY 10010

Developed and produced for Rosen by BlueApple*Works* Inc.

Creative Director: Melissa McClellan
Managing Editor for BlueApple*Works*: Melissa McClellan
Designer: T.J. Choleva
Photo Research: Jane Reid
Editor: Marcia Abramson
Craft Artisans: Janet Kompare-Fritz (p. 14); Sarah Hodgins (p. 18, 20, 28); Jane Yates (p. 8, 16 , 24);
Jerrie McClellan (p. 10, 12, 22, 26)

Photo Credits: cover center image Africa Studio/Shutterstock; cover background image, title page background Ocskay
Bence/Shutterstock; cover insets, title page, TOC, p. 6 bottom, 8–9, 10–11, 12–13, 14–15, 16–17, 18–19, 20–21, 22–23,
24–25, 26–27, 28-29, 30 Austen Photography; p. 4 left, 5 first row Photka/Dreamstime; p. 4 right Ermolaevamariya/
Dreamstime; p. 4 right bottom Richard Thomas/Dreamstime; p. 5 first row right Ghassan Safi/Dreamstime; p. 5 second
row left Design56/Dreamstime; p. 5 second row middle Christian Bertrand/Dreamstime; p. 5 second row right Fuse/
Thinkstock; p. 5 third row left Vasily Kovalev/Dreamstime; p. 5 third row middle Sergey Mostovoy/Dreamstime; p. 5
third row right (left to right) Crackerclips/Dreamstime; Les Cunliffe/Dreamstime; Jerryb8/Dreamstime; p. 5 fourth row
left Romval/Dreamstime; p. 5 fourth row right (left to right clockwise) Arinahabich08/Dreamstime; antpkr/Thinkstock;
Kelpfish/Dreamstime; Jirk4/Dreamstime; Gradts/Dreamstime; sodapix sodapix/Thinkstock; p. 6 top Jakub Krechowicz/
Dreamstime; p. 6 middle Steveheap/Dreamstime; p. 7 top Konstantin Kirillov/Dreamstime; p. 9 top right Africa Studio/
Shutterstock; p. 11 bottom left Jose Manuel Gelpi Diaz/Dreamstime; p. 11 top right 4x6/iStockphoto; p. 13 top right
Dr Ajay Kumar Singh/Shutterstock; p. 15 top right Serrnovik/Dreamstime; p. 17 top right Rossco/Dreamstime; p.
19 top right Milosluz/Dreamstime; p. 21 top right Monkey Business Images/Shutterstock; p. 23 top right Thomas
Vieth/Dreamstime; p. 25 top right Alekosa/Dreamstime; p. 27 top right Srki66/Dreamstime; p. 29 top right Claudia
Paulussen/Shutterstock

Cataloging-in-Publication Data
Names: Yates, Jane.
Title: Cool crafts with cloth / Jane Yates.
Description: New York : Windmill Books, 2018. | Series: Don't throw it away...craft it! | Includes index.
Identifiers: ISBN 9781499482874 (pbk.) | ISBN 9781499482812 (library bound) | ISBN 9781499482621 (6 pack)
Subjects: LCSH: Textile crafts--Juvenile literature. | Salvage (Waste, etc.)--Juvenile literature. | Handicraft--
   Juvenile literature.
Classification: LCC TT712.Y38 2018 | DDC 746--dc23

Manufactured in the United States of America
CPSIA Compliance Information: Batch #BS17WM For Further Information contact: Rosen Publishing, New York, New York at 1-800-237-9932

CONTENTS

GETTING STARTED

Have fun while making your cloth crafts! Be creative. Your craft projects do not have to look just like the ones in this book. You can reuse old clothes by making them into crafts. Use up odd socks and old T-shirts. You can even use leftover buttons! Save scraps of material and felt when making other crafts. Rather than throwing them out, these scraps can be used in another project. Save stuffing from old toys or discarded pillows. You can also make your own stuffing by using cut-up strips of plastic bags.

Any project in the book requiring scissors, needles, or pins should be made with adult supervision. Be very careful when using sharp instruments.

RECYCLABLES

You can make all of the crafts in this book with materials found around the house. Along with fabric, save recyclables (newspapers, cardboard, cans, bottles, magazines, gift wrap, cards, and more) to use in your craft projects. Use your imagination and have fun!

A note about measurements

Measurements are given in U.S. form with metric in parentheses. The metric conversion is rounded to the nearest whole number to make it easier to measure.

THREAD

RULER

SCISSORS

SEWING NEEDLES

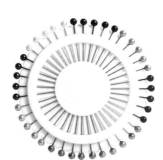

GLUE AND TAPE

STUFFING

SEWING PINS

SAFETY PINS

STIR STICKS

YARN

PENCIL

CRAFT WIRE

BUTTONS

FELT

RIBBON

Lightweight aluminum craft wire that can be cut with scissors

5

TECHNIQUES

Use the following techniques to create your cloth crafts.

THREADING A NEEDLE

● Use a tapestry needle for working with yarn. Use a needle with a smaller opening for working with thread.

● Wet one end of the thread in your mouth. Poke it through the needle opening. Pull some of the thread through until you have an even amount and make a double knot.

● For yarn, fold a piece of yarn over, then push the fold through the opening. This is easier than using a single thread.

Put the thread through the loop.

Fold the yarn, then feed it through the loop.

USING PATTERNS

● Patterns help you cut out exact shapes when sewing.

● Use tape or pins to attach the pattern to the cloth before you start cutting.

● When cutting out a shape, cut around the shape first, then make smaller cuts.

● When cutting with scissors, move the piece of cloth instead of the scissors.

● Make sure you keep your fingers out of the way while cutting. Ask an adult for help if needed.

Trace the pattern.

Cut the pattern out.

Attach the pattern to the cloth.

Cut the cloth along the pattern lines.

RUNNING STITCH

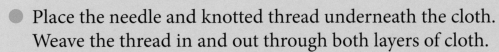

- Use a running stitch to sew one piece of cloth on top of another piece.
- Thread a needle, then tie a knot at the other end.
- Place the needle and knotted thread underneath the cloth. Weave the thread in and out through both layers of cloth.
- Continue stitching until finished.
- When you are done sewing, tie a knot on the back of the cloth to hold the stitches in place.

OVERCAST STITCH

- Thread a needle, then tie a knot at the other end.
- Place the needle and knotted thread in between the two pieces of cloth. Push the needle through the top layer. Pull the thread through so the knot is hidden in between the layers.
- Loop the needle around the edges of the cloth. Push the needle through both layers of cloth to make your first full stitch.
- Angle the needle toward the spot where the next stitch will be.
- Continue stitching until finished.

BACKSTITCH

The diagram below is enlarged to show you the movements and steps of this stitch. Your stitches will be much closer together.

- Starting in the position where the number one is on the diagram, take a needle with knotted thread and bring it up through the **wrong side** (the back) of the fabric. Make a stitch by pushing the needle down and through the fabric where the number two is.

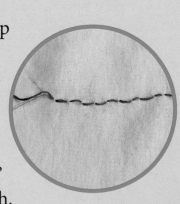

- Bring the needle back up a space away from the first stitch, where the number three is, and down at the end of that stitch, where the number four is. This is the "back" part. Continue the pattern. This makes a very strong stitch.

YOU'LL NEED:

- Old necktie
- Scissors
- Craft wire
- Duct tape
- Stuffing material
- Pencil
- Glue (that dries clear)
- Felt scraps
- Googly eyes

DID YOU KNOW?

A silkworm spins its cocoon from a single thread of raw silk that can be as long as 0.6 mile (1 km). Neckties often are made of this natural silk.

Tie Snake

Make a bendable stuffed snake with an old necktie. In cold climates, people often put snakes like these along the bottom of doors to keep out drafts.

1 If the bottom end of the tie is stitched closed, cut the stitches to open it up.

2 Have an adult cut a piece of craft wire slightly shorter than the tie. (You could also use a thin wire hanger.) Insert it into the tie so it goes from end to end.

3 Using two small pieces of duct tape for each end, tape the wire to the tie.

4 Stuff the tie with a small amount of stuffing. Use a pencil to help stuff it down the tie. Glue the opening closed after you have added the stuffing.

5 Cut eyes and a tongue from felt scraps. Glue googly eyes to the felt eyes. Glue the eyes to the snake. Pose the snake into whatever shape you want.

You can make a caterpillar if you don't like snakes. Cut one leg off of an old pair of tights. Insert the wire and stuffing. Tie the open end closed with a piece of string. Tie off sections with more pieces of string. Trim the ends of the string. Add felt eyes and a mouth.

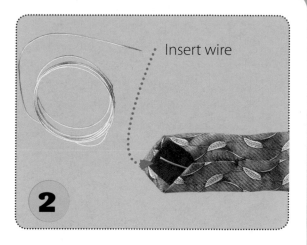

Insert wire

2

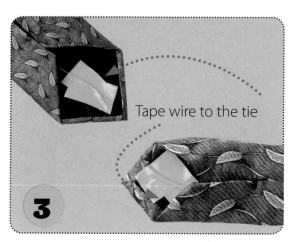

Tape wire to the tie

3

Glue

4

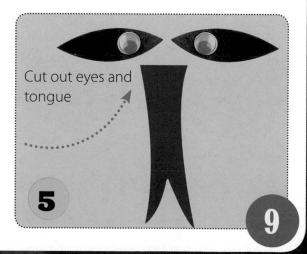

Cut out eyes and tongue

5

9

- Paper and pencil
- Scissors
- Old shirts, jeans, felt, or cotton scraps
- Light color marker
- Safety pins
- Needle and thread
- Stuffing
- Ribbon
- Glue (that dries clear)

10

Ornaments

Fabric scraps can become ornaments for your valentine or any celebration.

1 Make paper patterns. Draw a heart or trace the heart on page 30. Cut the pattern out.

2 Cut out two pieces of fabric that are bigger than the pattern. Place them together with the **right sides** facing out. Place the pattern on top and trace around the pattern with a light color marker.

3 Pin the fabric together. Stitch along the shape using a running stitch. Leave a small opening.

4 Stuff in a small amount of stuffing through the opening.

5 Continue sewing until the opening is closed. Tie off and cut the remaining thread. Cut around the stitching leaving a 0.5-inch (1 cm) edge. (Optional: Cut fringe around the edge.)

6 Cut a small piece of ribbon and attach to the top of the ornament with a few stitches or glue. Cut a smaller heart from another piece of fabric and glue to the front of the ornament.

Create a **bunting** to celebrate someone's special day. Draw the letters and ornament shapes on paper and follow the steps above. Attach the letters and ornaments to a long piece of ribbon with mini-clothespins.

2 Trace around the pattern

3 Sew along the line

5 Cut around the stitching

6 Stitch the ribbon to the back

11

YOU'LL NEED:

- Cardboard
- Scissors
- Yarn
- Tapestry needle
- White felt
- 2 buttons or googly eyes
- Needle and thread
- Pencil and paper
- Card stock or construction paper

1 Wrap

2 Tie

3 Cut

Sock Puppet

People have been making sock puppets since at least the 1920s. It's a great way to reuse a sock with no mate.

1 Cut a piece of cardboard 6 inches (15 cm) wide. Wind yarn around the cardboard about 50 times. Cut the end.

2 Cut a 12-inch (30 cm) piece of yarn and tie it around the center of the yarn loop.

3 Turn the cardboard over. Cut the yarn loop in the center of the board opposite the knot on the front of the board.

4 Attach the hair to the sock. Thread each end of the piece of yarn you tied around the others on a tapestry needle and pull them through the sock near the toe end. Tie the two yarn ends together and make a double knot.

5 Cut circles out of felt using the pattern on page 30. Sew buttons or glue googly eyes to the circles. Glue the circles to the sock.

6 Trace the pattern on page 30 for the glasses. Cut out the pattern. Trace the outline onto a piece of scrap card stock or construction paper.

7 Cut out the glasses. Poke a hole in the center of each eye piece and then cut out the square opening. Poke a hole with a needle at the end of each side piece and sew to the sock.

Make a whole cast of characters from socks and put on a puppet show.

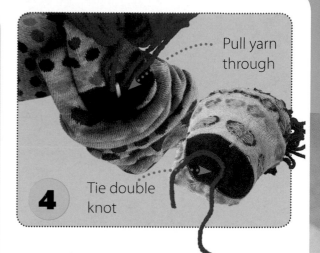

4 Pull yarn through

Tie double knot

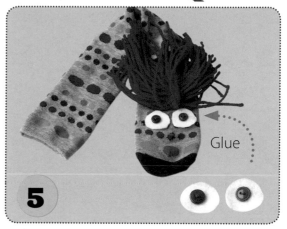

5 Glue

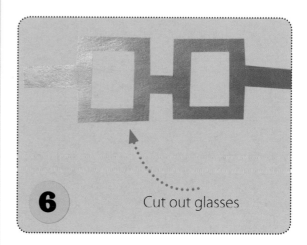

6 Cut out glasses

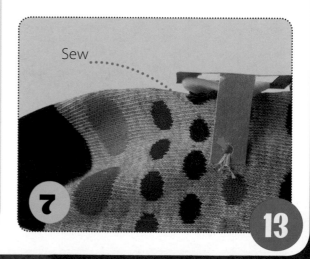

Sew

7

DID YOU KNOW?

Using cloth bags saves material and energy because fewer plastic bags need to be made. It also helps keep plastic out of landfills and water sources. Plastic bags kill many birds and other animals each year, so it's safer for them too.

Book Bag

When you outgrow a T-shirt, turn it into a colorful bag for carrying books or other items.

1 Decorate an old white T-shirt with markers.

2 Use a bowl as a guide and draw a circle around the neck.

3 Cut out the circle around the neck. Cut the sleeves off.

4 Turn the T-shirt inside out. Smooth it out on a flat surface. Cut fringes about 3 inches (8 cm) long along the bottom hem. Cut through both layers.

5 Tie the fringes together. See page 31 for detailed instructions.

6 Turn the bag right side out so you can see your decorations and the fringes are hidden.

The size of the T-shirt will determine the size of the bag. Make a bag with a small T-shirt too. If you have a T-shirt with a logo or design you love, you can use that to make a bag too. Just skip the decorating step.

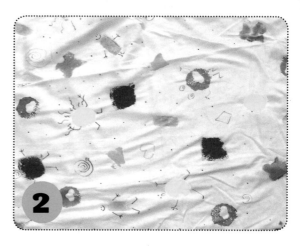
2

*Cut
3

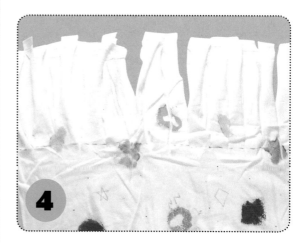
4

5

15

YOU'LL NEED:

- **Scrap fabric or old T-shirt**
- **Scissors**
- **Paper and pencil**
- **Glue (that dries clear)**
- **Brush for glue**
- **Buttons**
- **Stir sticks or craft sticks**
- **Markers or ribbon**

DID YOU KNOW?

Charities sell only about 10 percent of donated clothing in thrift shops. These clothes are usually in good condition. Large recycling companies buy the rest. A lot of these clothes become new products, but about 25 percent of them are sold for people in developing countries to wear.

Fabric Flowers

These fabric flowers make a great gift for Mother's Day or for a teacher.

1 Lay the fabric flat on a table. If you are using an old T-shirt, cut the sleeves off. Cut the fabric into squares.

2 Trace the pattern from page 30. Cut the paper into a square. Use a brush to coat the back of the paper with glue. Press it onto the wrong side of the fabric square. Press on it with your hand to smooth it out.

3 With the pattern facing you, cut along the line. Turn the flower over and glue a button to the center of the flower. As the glue dries, it will make the petals curl out.

4 Make stems from stir sticks or craft sticks. Decorate them by coloring them with markers. You can also glue fabric or a piece of ribbon to them.

5 Glue or tape the stem to the back of the flower. Make leaves by following step 2 and using the pattern on page 30. Glue to the decorated stick.

Make a vase for your flowers by covering a glass jar with glue. Press fabric scraps into the glue. Once the jar is covered with fabric, coat it with another layer of glue. Let the glue dry.

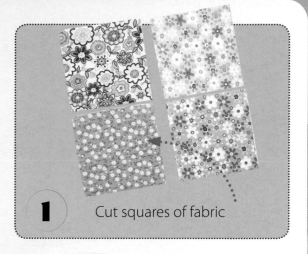

1 Cut squares of fabric

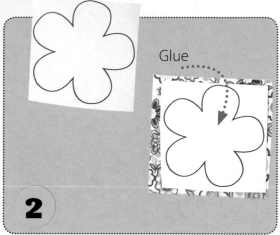

Glue

2

Glue

3

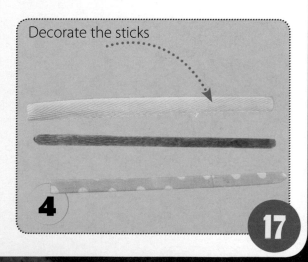

Decorate the sticks

4

YOU'LL NEED:

- Journal or notebook
- Old jeans
- Ruler and marker
- Scissors
- White glue
- Ribbon

DID YOU KNOW?

Americans donate or recycle only 15 percent of their clothing. About 13 million tons (12 million metric tons) of old clothes go into landfills every year.

1
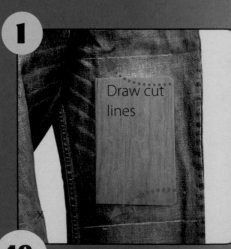
Draw cut lines

2

3

Draw cut lines ··········

journal Cover

Covering journals or notebooks protects them. When you make a cover from old jeans, you even get a handy pocket.

1 Place your journal on one leg of the jeans. Using a ruler, measure 2 inches (5 cm) above and below your journal. Draw a line across so you know where to cut. Cut along the two lines. Trim off the thick seam along the edge before going any further.

2 Open up the fabric and place the spine of your journal in the center of your jean fabric.

3 Using a ruler, measure 2 inches (5 cm) all around the journal and draw straight lines. Jeans are never quite straight so you need to make sure that the piece you cut is equal all around the journal. Cut around the straight lines.

4 Glue the top and bottom first. Apply white glue to the top and bottom of the seam fabric. Fold it over so that 2 inches (5 cm) is glued down. Give the glue some time to dry.

5 Place your journal down, glue the 2 inches (5 cm) on each side, and fold it over to glue it to the inside of your journal. Give the glue some time to dry.

6 Cut out one of the pockets from the jeans. Glue the pocket onto the front of your journal.

7 Measure the length of the seam on the inside cover of your journal. Cut two pieces of ribbon the same length. Glue them down along the edge of the jean fabric. This makes a nice edge. Cut two more pieces to glue over the pocket seams on the front of the cover.

You can also try other materials from different old clothes. The process is exactly the same!

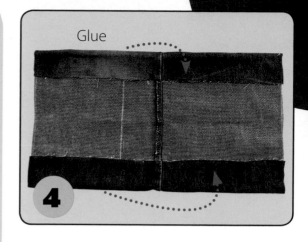

Glue

4

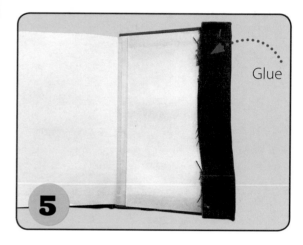

Glue

5

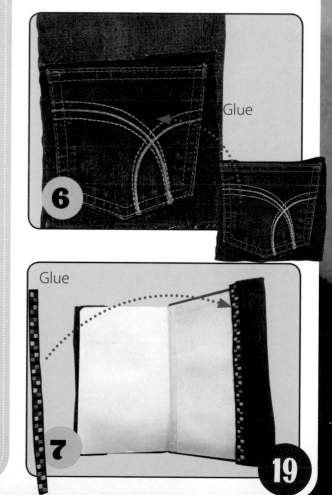

Glue

6

Glue

7

- **Tracing paper or newspaper**
- **Pencil and ruler**
- **Scissors**
- **T-shirt for the main pillow form**
- **Sewing pins**
- **Extra T-shirt or scrap fabric for the appliqué**
- **Embroidery thread and needle**
- **Ribbon**
- **Needle and thread**
- **Stuffing**
- **Optional: Sewing machine**

1

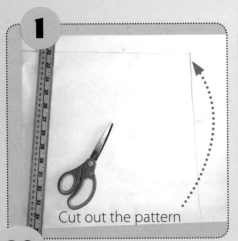

Cut out the pattern

2

Pin the pattern to the T-shirt

3

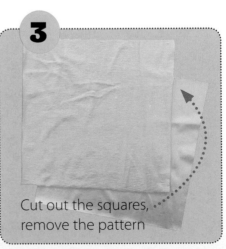

Cut out the squares, remove the pattern

T-shirt Pillow

Old T-shirts make soft, comfy pillows.

1 Using tracing paper or newspaper and a ruler, create a 13-inch (33 cm) square. This will produce a 12-inch (30 cm) square pillow with a 1-inch (3 cm) **seam allowance**.

2 Cut the square out and place it on the body of the T-shirt. Pin it in place so that it doesn't move while you are cutting around the square.

3 Cut around the square through both layers of the T-shirt. You will now have two equal pieces. These are the front and the back of the pillow.

4 Fold another piece of tracing paper or newspaper in half. Using the folded end as the base, draw a triangle on the paper. The size is up to you, but the shape you cut out will need to fit on one side of the pillow. Cut along the two lines you drew. When you unfold the paper, you will have a kite shape. Pin it to your extra T-shirt or fabric and cut around the shape.

5 Pin the kite shape onto the front square of your pillow. Using embroidery thread and a needle, stitch the kite shape to the front of the pillow. Use an overcast stitch, which goes over the edge of the kite shape, to hold it in place.

6 With a pencil, lightly draw the string of the kite on the front of your pillow. Using embroidery thread, sew along the shape of the string you drew. Use a backstitch for this so it fills up the whole line you drew.

7 Cut 6 pieces of ribbon about 2 inches (5 cm) each in length. Cross two ribbons together and using the embroidery thread, sew them down on the kite string. Repeat this for the other 4 ribbon pieces. This will create 3 bows on your kite string.

8 Now you are ready to put your pillow together. See page 31 for instructions.

Remember, you can come up with your own designs for the appliqué. You can also use an old T-shirt with logos and just sew the pillow together!

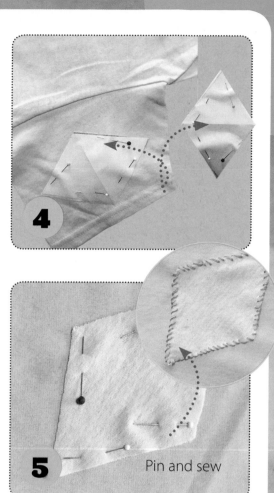

4

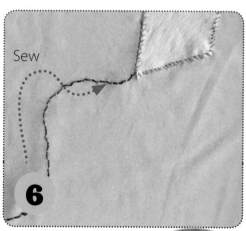

5 Pin and sew

Sew

6

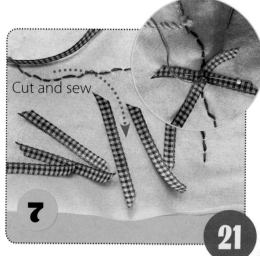

Cut and sew

7

DID YOU KNOW?

When clothing arrives at the recycling center, it is first sorted and shredded. Once that is done, clothing and other fabrics can be formed into many products, including insulation, carpet padding, yarn, paper, and even stuffing for toys!

Rag Wreath

Match the colors of a rag wreath to the season. Use floral fabrics for spring or red and green for Christmas.

1 Bend craft wire or a wire clothes hanger into a circle.

2 Make a hook at the top before wrapping the remaining wire around the circle to secure it.

3 Make a template for cutting out the fabric. Cut a piece of thin cardboard in a rectangle 1.5 inches (4 cm) wide by 6 inches (15 cm) long.

4 Use the cardboard template as a guide to cut out fabric strips. The pieces do not have to be exactly the same size. You may want to arrange the strips into piles of colors. Cut out 25 strips to start then more as you need them.

5 Tie the fabric strip around the wire and open the ends to look like a bow tie.

6 Continue wrapping scraps until the wire is full. The tighter you pack the strips, the fuller the wreath will look.

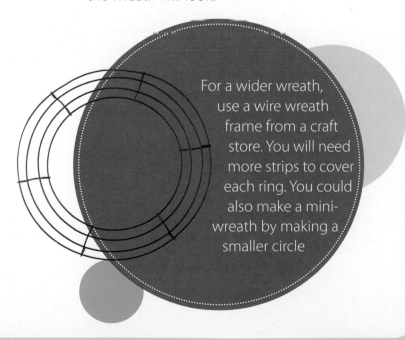

For a wider wreath, use a wire wreath frame from a craft store. You will need more strips to cover each ring. You could also make a mini-wreath by making a smaller circle

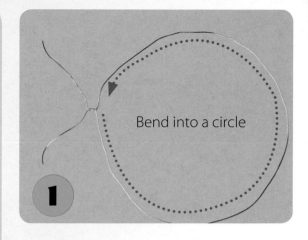

1 Bend into a circle

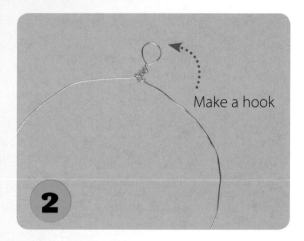

Make a hook

2

Cut many strips

4

Tie the strips to the frame

5

23

YOU'LL NEED:

- Tracing paper or newspaper
- Ruler and pencil
- Scissors
- Old fleece pants or pajamas
- Safety pins

DID YOU KNOW?

Many areas have curbside recycling for clothing and other fabrics. Others have donation or recycling boxes where you can drop off used clothing. Some charities also pick up clothing or have drop-off centers. No matter where you live, there should be a way to keep clothing out of the landfill!

Fleece Scarf

Old fleece pants or pajamas can be turned into warm scarves. They make thoughtful gifts for the winter holidays.

1 Using tracing paper or newspaper and a ruler, draw a 7-inch (18 cm) by 16-inch (41 cm) rectangle. Cut it out.

2 Pin the rectangles in place along the pant or pajama leg.

3 Cut along the pattern. When you get to the end of the pattern, unpin it and repin it above where you stopped cutting. Cut again.

4 Cut fringes at each end of the scarf.

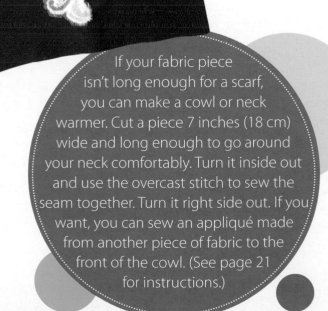

If your fabric piece isn't long enough for a scarf, you can make a cowl or neck warmer. Cut a piece 7 inches (18 cm) wide and long enough to go around your neck comfortably. Turn it inside out and use the overcast stitch to sew the seam together. Turn it right side out. If you want, you can sew an appliqué made from another piece of fabric to the front of the cowl. (See page 21 for instructions.)

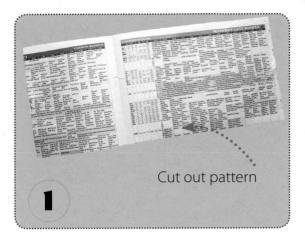

1 Cut out pattern

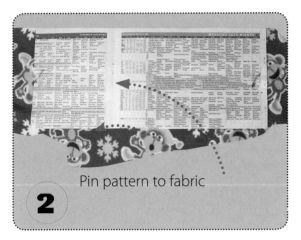

2 Pin pattern to fabric

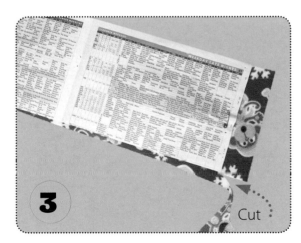

3 Cut

4 Cut fringe

- Raffia or corn husks
- Duct tape
- Old pants and long-sleeved shirt
- Twine
- 2 old T-shirts
- Safety pins
- Wire clothes hanger
- Plastic plate or aluminum pie plate
- Stuffing
- Markers
- Bandana
- Old hat
- Pole, stick, or long cardboard tube

1 ······· Tape

2 ······· Tie

3

······· Tie

Scarecrow

Welcome fall and Halloween by making a scarecrow to hang up outside.

1 Arrange four sections of raffia or corn husks. Gather each into a cluster and tape one end together. Two of the sections should be bigger than the other two.

2 Insert the two large ones into the pant legs. Cut two pieces of twine. Wrap each piece around a pant leg and tie and knot the twine.

3 Insert the two small sections of husk into the end of the sleeves of the long-sleeved shirt. Cut two pieces of twine. Wrap each piece around a sleeve and tie and knot the twine.

4 Use safety pins to secure the bottom of the first T-shirt to the top of the pants.

5 Tape a hanger to the back of a plastic plate. Tape some stuffing material to the front of the plate. Put the plastic plate inside the second T-shirt. Gather and use safety pins or tape to secure the shirt to the back of the plate.

6 Use markers to draw a face on the second T-shirt. Tie a bandana under the head.

7 Hang the shirt with pants attached on the hanger. Tie twine through the belt loops for a belt. Place the long-sleeved shirt over the body T-shirt.

8 Tape hair (raffia or dried corn husks) inside the hat and add to head.

9 Stick a pole, stick, or cardboard tube under the long-sleeved shirt and tape it to the back of the head.

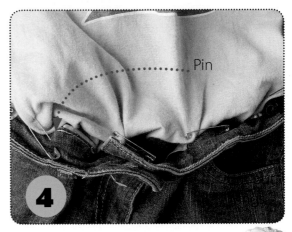

4 — Pin

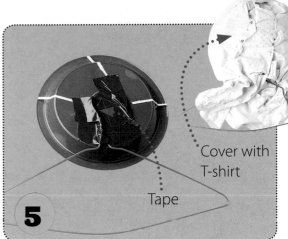

5 — Cover with T-shirt — Tape

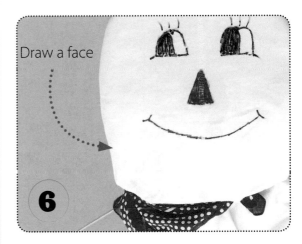

6 — Draw a face

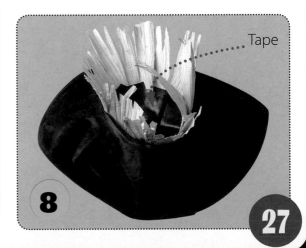

8 — Tape

YOU'LL NEED:

- Old pillowcase, shirt, or bedsheet. It must be a natural fiber like cotton.
- Ruler and pencil
- Scissors
- White glue
- Wax paper
- Fabric dye (we used ones included in a tie-dye kit for kids)
- Brush
- Water
- Card paper
- Hole punch
- Ribbon, yarn, or string

1

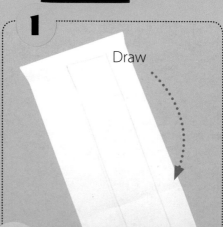

Draw

2

Draw

SAMMIE

3

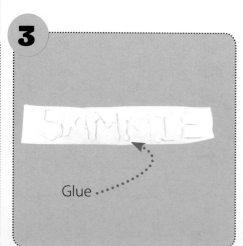

SAMMIE

Glue

Batik Bookmarks

Batik is an ancient design technique from the island of Java. Use it to make unique bookmarks.

1 Using a pencil and ruler, measure your bookmark on your fabric. A good size is 7 inches (18 cm) long by 1.5 inches (4 cm) wide. Cut out your bookmark.

2 Make your design on the bookmark. If you want to draw your design first, use pencil to draw it in your bookmark.

3 Using white glue, go over your drawn designs. You can also make freehand and abstract designs straight on the bookmark with the white glue.

4 Dry your white glue design on wax paper overnight.

5 Mix up your fabric dye according to the instructions that came with it. It is good to have the three primary colors as those can make many colors when they mix and blend together.

6 Using water, a brush, and the fabric dye, brush the dye onto your bookmark. The more water that is added with your dye, the lighter the dye will be. It is good to start with lighter colors first. Let your dyed bookmark dry overnight.

7 Soak your bookmark in hot water. Let it sit in the hot water until the glue starts to soften and wash away from your fabric. Take the bookmark out of the water and let it fully dry.

8 Cut your card paper so that it is a little bit bigger than your bookmark. Glue your dry bookmark to the paper.

9 Use a hole punch to make a hole at the top of your bookmark and tie some ribbon, yarn, or string at the top to decorate the bookmark.

5

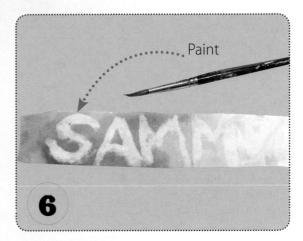

Paint

6

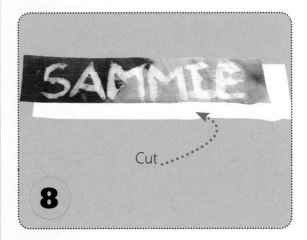

SAMMIE

Cut

8

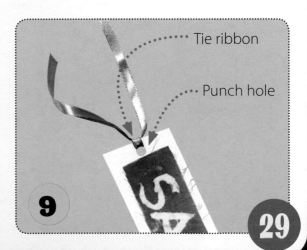

Tie ribbon

Punch hole

9

PATTERNS

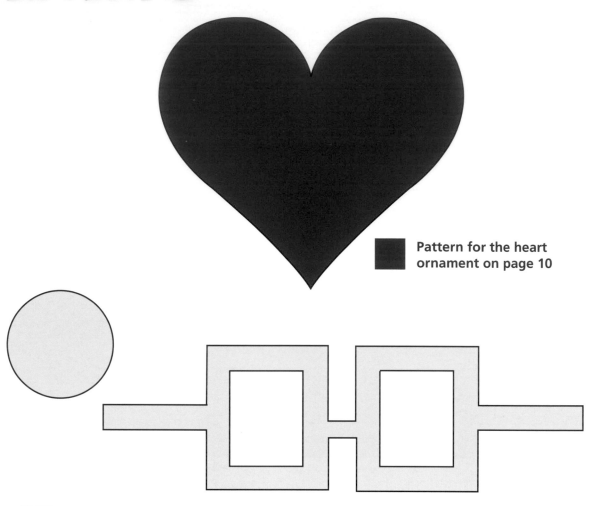

Pattern for the heart
ornament on page 10

Pattern for the eyes and glasses on page 12

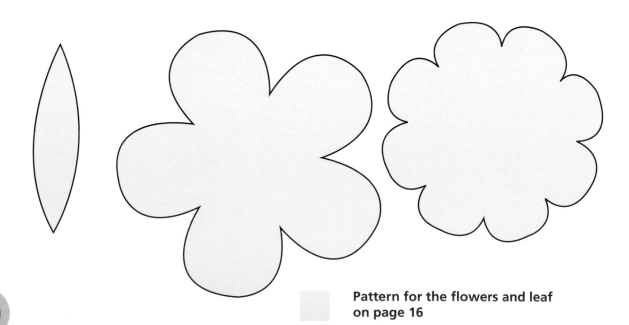

Pattern for the flowers and leaf
on page 16

Instructions for knotting book bag fringe on page 14

(Note: the diagram below is meant to help you understand the basic movements of this step. Your project will not look exactly like this.)

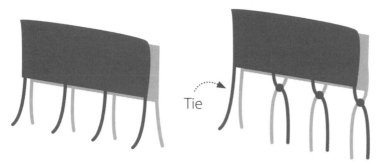

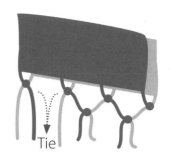

You should have cut fringe on both the front and the back of what was your T-shirt. Each piece of fringe should line up with a piece on the other side of the fabric. To close up the bottom of the bag, you need to tie each piece of fringe with the piece across from it. Tie the knots tightly so the two sides of the bag close together. Each group of two fringes you have tied together is called a pair.

There are still holes between each pair you've knotted together. To fix this, you need to tie the pairs together. Starting from the left, tie one piece of fringe from the first pair to one piece of fringe from the second pair. Make sure to knot the pieces tightly so there aren't any holes at the bottom of your bag. Then tie the other fringe from the second pair to one fringe of the third pair. Next, tie the other fringe of the third pair to one fringe of the fourth pair. Follow this pattern until you have tied every pair together.

Instructions for sewing the pillow on page 20

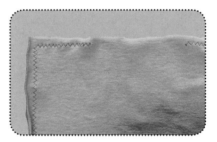

Place the front and back pillow pieces together. Make sure the appliqué is facing to the inside. Pin the pieces together. Make sure you leave an opening on the bottom of your pillow. Leave enough space to put your hand in to fill the pillow with stuffing.

You can sew around the edges by hand with a needle and thread or you can use a sewing machine. If you use a sewing machine, choose a zigzag stitch as it makes the edge more stretchy just like the t-shirt fabric you are using! Remember not to sew the opening on the bottom that you left to fill the pillow with stuffing.

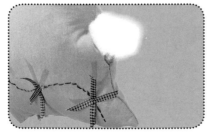

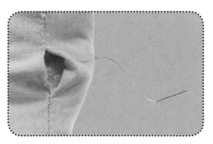

Once your pillow is sewn, turn it right side out and fill with stuffing.

Sew up the bottom hole that you left for the stuffing.

GLOSSARY

appliqué Small decorations sewn onto fabric.

batik A way to make designs while dyeing fabric by blocking out areas with wax.

bunting Banner made of cloth.

right side The printed or top side of fabric.

seam allowance The area between the edge of the fabric and the stitching.

wrong side The underside or nonprinted side of fabric.

FOR MORE INFORMATION

FURTHER READING

Akass, Susan. *My First Sewing Book: 35 Easy and Fun Projects for Children Aged 7 Years +*. New York: CICO Books, 2011.

Cherry, Winky. *My First Sewing Book: Hand Sewing*. Vancouver, WA: Palmer/Pletsch Publishing, 2011.

Lisle, Andria. *Sewing School: 21 Sewing Projects Kids Will Love to Make*. North Adams, MA: Storey Publishing, 2010.

WEBSITES

For web resources related to the subject of this book, go to: **www.windmillbooks.com/weblinks** and select this book's title.

INDEX